An Orange Tree Theatre, Actor
Theatre Royal Plymouth produ[

AMSTE[   ]

by Maya Arad Yasur
translated by **Eran Edry**

Cast
Daniel Abelson
Fiston Barek
Michal Horowicz
Hara Yannas

Direction **Matthew Xia**
Design **Naomi Kuyck-Cohen**
Movement **Jennifer Jackson**
Lighting **Ciarán Cunningham**
Sound **Max Pappenheim**
Casting Consultant **Sophie Parrott CDG**
Assistant Director **Georgia Green**

Production Manager **Lisa Hood**
Production Technician **Rhea Jacques**
Stage Manager **Caoimhe Regan**
Deputy Stage Manager **Sylvia Darkwa Ohemeng**
Assistant Stage Manager **Stevie Wren**
Costume Supervisor **Rianna Azoro**
Production LX **Tom Turner**

Thanks to Roehampton University production department,
Teunkie Van Der Sluijs and Marie-Ange Camara

UK premiere at the Orange Tree Theatre on 6 September 2019

DANIEL ABELSON

Daniel Abelson's work in theatre includes *Circa* (Old Red Lion); *The Rivals* (Watermill); *William Wordsworth* (ETT/Theatre by the Lake); *Once in a Lifetime* (Young Vic); *The Mighty Waltzer* (Royal Exchange Theatre); *A Midsummer Night's Dream*, *The Comedy of Errors* (Sprite Productions); *A Midsummer Night's Dream* (Opera North); *Me, As A Penguin* (Arcola/Lowry/West Yorkshire Playhouse); *Country Magic* (Finborough); *Goodbye My Love* (Southwark Playhouse); *Macbeth* (West Yorkshire Playhouse); *Shadow of a Gunman* (Citizens Theatre, Glasgow); *5/11, King Lear, The Government Inspector, A Midsummer Night's Dream, Seven Doors, Thermidor, The Seagull* and *Holes in the Skin* (Chichester Festival Theatre).

TV includes *Jonathan Pie's American Pie, Humans, Law & Order UK, Coronation Street, EastEnders, I Shouldn't Be Alive, Doctors, The Royal Today* and *Robin Hood*.

Film includes *The Rack Pack*.

FISTON BAREK

Fiston Barek trained at ALRA.

His work in theatre includes *The Rolling Stone* (Orange Tree Theatre/ Royal Exchange Theatre); *King Lear* (The Old Vic); *Routes* and *Truth and Reconciliation* (Royal Court); *Little Baby* Jesus (Oval House); *Love the Sinner* (National Theatre).

TV includes *Silent Witness, Holby City* and *Doctors*.

Film includes *TAU* (Netflix), *After Love* and *Don't Look Back*.

MICHAL HOROWICZ

Michal Horowicz trained at the Royal Central School of Speech and Drama.

Theatre includes: *Neverland* (Hartshorn-Hook/Guild of Misrule/Theatre Deli); *The Famous Five* (Gobbledigook Theatre); *Mimi and the Mountain Dragon* (Skewbald Theatre); *Bylines* (Theatre 503); *Resources of Quinola* (The Cockpit); *The Winter's Tale* (Minack Theatre).

TV includes *Tikva* and *Saving the Forgotten Jews*.

HARA YANNAS

Theatre includes: *Dealing with Clair* (Orange Tree Theatre/ETT); *Uncle Vanya* (HOME, Manchester); *The Treatment, The House of Bernarda Alba* (Almeida); *Oresteia* (Almeida/Trafalgar Studios); *1984* (Headlong tour/Almeida/West End/US Tour); *Mare Rider* (Arcola); *Britannicus* (Wilton's Music Hall); *Pericles* (Open Air Theatre, Regent's Park); *Uncle Vanya* (Arcola/Belgrade, Coventry); *Tales of the Harrow Road* (Soho Theatre); *A Midsummer Night's Dream* (Shakespeare's Globe/UK & European tour); *it felt empty when the heart went at first but it is alright now* (Arcola/Clean Break).

TV includes: *Silent Witness, Dark Heart, Trauma, Innocent, Broadchurch, The Level, Father Brown, The Musketeers, Law & Order: UK, The Smoke, The Bible* and *Holby City*.

MAYA ARAD YASUR
Writer

Maya Arad Yasur (1976) holds a Master's degree in Dramaturgy from the University of Amsterdam where she graduated with distinction. Her plays were staged and publically read in various theatres in Israel, Germany, Austria, Norway, France and the U.S. and were published in leading theatre magazines in Germany, Poland, China and Israel. Maya is the recipient of the Berliner TheaterTreffen Stückemarkt prize 2018 for *Amsterdam*, the 1st prize of the international playwriting competition of ITI–UNESCO 2011 for Suspended and the Habima (Israel's National Theatre) Prize for emerging artists 2014 for *God Waits at the Station*.
Her new play *Bomb* will premiere in Schauspiel Cologne in season 19/20.

ERAN EDRY
Translator

Eran is a screenwriter, translator, and songwriter who has worked in international film, television, and theatre since 2005. From writing extensively for children's television (BabyFirstTV, Helen Doron Group, Zumbini) to his most recent collaborations with high-profile Israeli filmmakers such as Eran Riklis (*Spider in the Web*, 2019), the Paz Brothers (*The Golem*, 2018), and Savi Gabizon (*Longing*, 2017), Eran writes, translates and adapts screenplays from Hebrew to global, English-speaking markets. This is Eran's third-time collaboration with *Amsterdam* creator and playwright, Maya Arad-Yasur. Highlights of his other theatre credits include translating original plays by Israeli director Shay Pitowski (*The Oath*, 2019), up-and-coming playwright, Nili Lamdan (*Land of Onions and Honey*, 2019), and an original musical (*A Tale of Two Tails*, 2015) for which Eran had written both book and lyrics. Eran lives in London where he is currently writing his debut children's novel and a television drama pilot.

MATTHEW XIA
Direction

This is Matthew Xia's first production as Artistic Director of Actors Touring Company (ATC). He recently directed *Blood Knot* at the Orange Tree Theatre, *One Night in Miami* at Nottingham Playhouse, and *Eden* at Hampstead Theatre. He won the Genesis Future Director award with his production of *Sizwe Banzi is Dead* at the Young Vic, where he also directed *Blue/Orange*. He was previously Associate Artistic Director at the Royal Exchange Theatre, where he directed *Brink, Into the Woods* and *Wish List*, which transferred to the Royal Court Theatre. In 2018 Matthew directed Conor McPherson's *Dublin Carol* at the Sherman Theatre in Cardiff, a new adaptation of *Frankenstein* by April de Angelis at the Royal Exchange, and *Shebeen*: Mufaro Makubika's Alfred Fagon Award-winning play at Nottingham Playhouse and Theatre Royal Stratford East, and *Sleeping Beauty* at Theatre Royal Stratford East, where he was previously Associate Director. He is a co-founder of Act for Change.

NAOMI KUYCK-COHEN
Design
Naomi Kuyck-Cohen is a Designer for performance. She also Co-Designs work with Lighting Designer Joshua Gadsby.

Co-Designs include: *There Is A Light That Never Goes Out: Scenes From The Luddite Rebellion* (Royal Exchange Theatre), *Trap Street* (Schaubühne and New Diorama), Dinomania (New Diorama), *Dreamplay* (The Vaults). Designs include: *The Greatest Play In The History Of The World* (Royal Exchange Theatre and Traverse Theatre), *And Yet It Moves* (Young Vic), *Nightclubbing* (European Tour), *OUT* (European Tour), *The Tempest (*Royal Exchange Theatre Young Company), *Fuck You Pay Me* (The Bunker), *The Sandman and What Was Left* (Southwark Playhouse), *Trigger Warning* (Tate Modern & UK tour), *In My Dreams I Dream I'm Dreaming* (Theatre Royal Plymouth), *Passin' Thru* (Lyric Hammersmith), *Feast* (Battersea Arts Centre).

JENNIFER JACKSON
Movement
Jennifer trained at East 15 and is a movement director and actor.

Movement direction includes: *Death of a Salesman, Our Town*

(Royal Exchange Theatre), *Queens of the Coal Age* (Royal Exchange & New Vic), *Parliament Square, Philoxenia, The Trick* (Bush Theatre/ Royal Exchange Theatre), *Out of Water, Mayfly* (Orange Tree), *Be My Baby, Around the World in Eighty Days* (Leeds Playhouse), *The Strange Undoing of Prudencia Hart* (The New Vic), T*he Mountaintop* (Young Vic & Tour), *Brighton Rock* (Pilot Theatre/The Lowry), *Big Aftermath of a Small Disclosure* (ATC), *Island Town, Sticks and Stones, How to Spot an Alien* (PainesPlough Roundabout), *Black Mountain, How to be a Kid, Out of Love* (Paines Plough/Orange Tree/Theatr Clwyd), *Death of a Salesman* (Royal & Derngate), *The Ugly One* (Park Theatre), *Why The Whales Came* (Southbank Centre), *Stone Face* (Finborough Theatre), *Debris* (Southwark Playhouse/Openworks Theatre), *Macbeth* (Passion in Practice/ Sam Wanamaker Playhouse), *Silent Planet* (Finborough), *Pericles* (Berwaldhallen), *The Future* (The Yard/Company Three), *Other-Please Specify, Atoms* (Company Three), *Takeover 2017* (Kiln Theatre). Assistant movement director: *Lungs, The Initiate, My Teacher's a Troll* (Paines Plough Roundabout 2014).

Jennifer is also a Leverhulme Arts Scholar, and is currently developing *Thank Heaven For Little Girls* with The egg, The Lowry and The Place.

CIARÁN CUNNINGHAM
Lighting
Ciarán Cunningham trained at East 15 Acting School.

Lighting Design Credits: *Blood Knot* (Orange Tree Theatre); *One Night In Miami* (Nottingham Playhouse Bristol Old Vic & Home,

Manchester); *Suckerpunch Boom Suite* (Barbican / Nitrobeat); *Eden* (Hampstead Theatre) ; *Sleeping Beauty* (Stratford Theatre Royal East); *Shebeen* (Nottingham Playhouse/Theatre Royal Stratford East); *Last Days Of Iscariot* (Vanbrugh Theatre); Dublin *Carol* (Sherman Theatre); *Into The Woods* and *Brink* (Royal Exchange Theatre); *Wish List* (Royal Exchange Theatre/Royal Court Theatre); *Sizwe Banzi Is Dead* (Young Vic/UK tour); *Sound Of Yellow* (Young Vic); *Sense Of Sound's: Migration Music* (Liverpool Everyman); *Scrappers* (Liverpool Playhouse); *In His Hands; Re:Definition And Collision* (Hackney Empire); *Blackout* (The Dukes Theatre); *The Mountaintop* (Welsh national tour); *Death And The Maiden* (The Other Room); *A Dream Cross The Ocean* (Fairfield Hall Ashcroft Theatre); *When Chaplin Met Gandhi* (Kingsley Hall); *Normal* (Rift); *Chris Dugdale: 2 Face Deception* (Leicester Square Theatre); *Letter To Larry* (Jermyn Street Theatre) and *The Flouers O'Edinburgh* (Finborough Theatre).

MAX PAPPENHEIM
Sound
Theatre includes *The Night of the Iguana* (Noel Coward Theatre); *The Way of the World* (Donmar); *The Children* (Royal Court/Broadway); *Dry Powder, Sex with Strangers, Labyrinth* (Hampstead); *Ophelias Zimmer* (Schaubühne, Berlin/Royal Court); *Macbeth* (Chichester Festival Theatre); *Crooked Dances* (RSC); *One Night in Miami* (Nottingham Playhouse); *Hogarth's Progress* (Rose, Kingston); *The Ridiculous Darkness* (Gate); *Humble Boy, Blue/Heart, The Distance* (Orange Tree); *The Gaul* (Hull Truck); *Cookies* (Theatre Royal Haymarket); *Jane Wenham* (Out of Joint); *Waiting for Godot* (Sheffield Crucible); *My Eyes Went Dark* (Traverse & 59E59, New York); *A Kettle of Fish* (Yard); *CommonWealth* (Almeida); *Creve Coeur* (Print Room); *Cuzco, Wink* (Theatre503); *Spamalot, The Glass Menagerie* (English Theatre, Frankfurt); *The Cardinal, Kiki's Delivery Service* (Southwark Playhouse); *Mrs Lowry and Son* (Trafalgar Studios); *Martine, Black Jesus, Somersaults* (Finborough); *The Habit of Art, Monogamy, Teddy, Toast, Fabric, Invincible* (National Tours).

Opera includes *Miranda* (Opéra Comique, Paris); *Scraww* (Trebah Gardens); *Vixen* (Vaults/International Tour); *Carmen:Remastered* (ROH/Barbican).

Radio includes *Home Front* (BBC Radio 4). Associate Artist of The Faction and Silent Opera.

SOPHIE PARROTT CDG
Casting Consultant
Theatre credits as Casting Director include: *Blood Knot, The March On Russia, An Octoroon* (Orange Tree Theatre); *An Octoroon, All the President's Men?, Pomona* (additional casting) (National Theatre); *Nora: A Doll's House* (Young Vic); *Rust* (Bush Theatre/ HighTide); *Songlines* (HighTide); *One Night In Miami, Shebeen, Wonderland* (re-mount) (Nottingham Playhouse); *The Crucible, Buggy Baby,*

This Beautiful Future (The Yard Theatre); *Big Aftermath of A Small Disclosure, Winter Solstice* (ATC); *Sweeney Todd, Paint Your Wagon, A Clockwork Orange, Othello, The Big I Am, A Midsummer Night's Dream* (Liverpool Everyman); *Old Fools* (Southwark Playhouse); *The Claim* (Shoreditch Town Hall/National Tour); *Death of a Salesman* (Royal & Derngate Northampton & Tour); *Wish List; Yen* (Royal Court/ Manchester Royal Exchange); *A Streetcar Named Desire* (co-casting director); *Britannia Waves the Rules* (tour), *Billy Liar* (Manchester Royal Exchange); *Bird* (Sherman Theatre, Cardiff/ Manchester Royal Exchange); *My Mother Said I Never Should* (St James Theatre); *The Crocodile* (Manchester International Festival).

Television and film credits as Casting Director include: *Call The Midwife* Series 9 (Neal Street Productions); *The Secret Agent* (O Som E A Fúria Films); *Doctors* (BBC).

Television and Film Credits as Casting Associate/ Assistant

include: *Britannia II, Delicious* (Sky); *Howards End, Rillington Place, Thirteen, Call the Midwife* (5 series), *The Game, Silent Witness* (3 series), *Esio Trot, The Night Watch, WPC56, Holby City* (4 series), *Mr Stink* (BBC); *A Street Cat Named Bob* (Streetcat Films).

GEORGIA GREEN
Assistant Director
Georgia Green is a director and playwright from London. Previous work as director includes The Mikvah Project at the Orange Tree, and short plays at Arcola, Theatre 503, Southwark Playhouse, Edinburgh and Camden Fringe.

As assistant: *Out of Water* and *The Double Dealer* at the Orange Tree.

As associate: *Zog* and *Tiddler and Other Terrific Tales* UK Tours. As a writer she has been part of writers groups at the Royal Court and Soho Theatre. She has facilitated for the Orange Tree, in schools and currently is directing a showcase for Identity School of Acting and has previously run the U18 Working with Text Course.

CAOIMHE REGAN
Stage Manager
Caoimhe has worked as a Stage Manager for more then 10 years.

Previous Orange Tree productions include: *The Double Dealer, An Octoroon* and *Out Of Water*.

Caoimhe has worked with many other theatre companies

which include include: ATC, Improbable, the National Theatre, Manchester International Festival, Theatre Lovett, the Royal Court, The Abbey Theatre, Prime Cut Productions, City Theatre Dublin, The Gate Theatre, Fishamble Theatre Company, THISISPOPBABY,

Pan Pan Theatre, HOME, Giant Events Company, The Ark Theatre, Broken Talkers, Junk Ensemble, Carpet Theatre Company, Performance Corporation, Druid Theatre Company, the Royal Exchange Theatre, WillFredd Theatre Company, Anu Productions, Gentle Giant Productions, Tall Tales Theatre Company, GoLightly Productions, Spark to a Flame Productions, Upstate Theatre Company, Landmark Productions, The Bryan Quinn Theatre Company, Spotlight Productions, C21 Theatre Company and HotForTheatre.

Caoimhe is the Company Stage Manager of The 24 Hour Plays Dublin.

SYLVIA DARKWA OHEMENG
Deputy Stage Manager
A Rose Bruford graduate in Stage Management, Sylvia has been working on productions such as *Estate Walls, Take a Deep Breath and Breathe, Grandfathers,* The 33% Festival (Creative Youth Department at Oval House); *24 Hour Plays* (Old Vic: New Voice); *Nine Rooms* (Old Vic Tunnels); The Lyric Lounge, Future Fest, *Eclipse* (NTC) The Lyric Hammersmith, *Grandfathers*(NTC), *When Women Wee* (Soho Theatre); *A Guide to Second Date Sex, Strong Arm* (Underbelly, Edinburgh Festival); *Ada Ada Ada* (Proximus Lounge, Brussels); *Brainstorm* (Temporary Space); *Putting Words in Your Mouth, Hive City Legacy* (Roundhouse); *Take-Over Season, Storylab* (Tricycle Theatre); NYT *Playing Up Season* (Arcola); *Halfbreed* (India tour), *Boys* (Vaults Festival); *Hijabi Monologues, Dismantle* (Bush Theatre); *Nine Night, Pericles* (National Theatre); *Barbershop Chronicles* (USA and Canada tour); *Richard II* (Shakespeare's Globe); *My White Best Friend and other stories* (Bunker Theatre); and *Seven Methods of Killing Kylie Jenner* (Royal Court Upstairs Theatre).

STEVIE WREN
Assistant Stage Manager
Stevie Wren is originally from Knaresborough, North Yorkshire and became part of the National Youth Theatre in 2014 where she worked on the NYT Productions at the Ambassadors Theatre in 2015. Following on from this she graduated from the London Academy of Music & Dramatic Art, completing her FdA in Stage Management and Technical Theatre in 2018. In 2017 Stevie also worked on *Un Ballo in Maschera* as an Assistant Stage Manager with Opera North as part of her time at LAMDA. She has gone on to Production Coordinate the LAMDA E2 Short Films (October 2018) and Deputy Stage Manage *Drag Me Out* (November 2018, Hen and Chicken Theatre, London). Earlier this year Stevie took on the role of Stage Manager for *This Island's Mine* at the King's Head Theatre where it is due to transfer to Trafalgar Studios early next year.

ORANGE TREE THEATRE

A powerhouse of independent theatre

The Orange Tree (OT) is an award-winning, independent theatre. Recognised as a powerhouse that creates high-quality productions of new and rediscovered plays, we entertain 70,000 people across the UK every year.

The OT's home in Richmond, South West London, is an intimate theatre with the audience seated all around the stage: watching a performance here is truly a unique experience.

We believe in the power of dramatic stories to entertain, thrill and challenge us; plays that enrich our lives by enhancing our understanding of ourselves and each other.

As a registered charity (266128) sitting at the heart of its community, we work with 10,000 people in Richmond and beyond through participatory theatre projects for people of all ages and abilities.

The Orange Tree Theatre's mission is to enable audiences to experience the next generation of theatre talent, experiment with ground-breaking new drama and explore the plays from the past that inspire the theatre-makers of the present. To find out how you can help us to do that you can visit **orangetreetheatre.co.uk/discover**

orangetreetheatre.co.uk

Registered charity no. 266128

ACTORS TOURING COMPANY

ATC's mission is to create dialogue between Britain and the rest of the world – and between the intersecting cultures within our country.

ATC is the only UK theatre company committed to producing plays that come from beyond our shores. We are also passionate about giving voice to the 'outsider within' – the intercultural nations within our own nation.

We tour our plays right across Britain: creating, developing and sustaining a dialogue between 'the other' and UK audiences. In an increasingly polarised society, we want to ensure that the international remains a vital part of the national conversation.

In the last few years, we have produced first English language productions of plays from Iran, Norway, the US, Germany, Austria, Russia - bringing international voices to school and village halls, studio theatres and main houses: from Barcelona to Glasgow, from Hong Kong to Scarborough.

Signature productions include: *The Brothers Size, The Events, The Suppliant Women, Winter Solstice* and the ATC debut of our new AD Matthew Xia, *Amsterdam*.

Can you help expand the reach and impact of ATC's work around the UK....?

Can you support our work with international writers, funding travel, ideas exchange and commissions?

Can you support our education packages for diverse participants across the UK?

Can you help us reach deeper and further into the UK, enabling UK audiences in areas of low engagement with the arts to experience international plays, and the voices of 'the other'?

BECOME A MEMBER
Member - £250 per year
Benefits include monthly newsletter, be the first to hear about new productions, drinks reception at one of our performances

Super Member - £500 or above per year
Benefits include the Members package, plus an invitation to Annual Artistic Director's dinner and the opportunity to observe rehearsals.

ONE-OFF DONATION
An easy-to-make donation of whatever amount you wish, using this link: www.atctheatre.com/support

Artistic Director: **Matthew Xia**
Executive Director: **Andrew Smaje**
General Manager: **Jess O'Connor**
Chair: **David Massarella**
PR: **David Burns**

Web: **www.atctheatre.com**
Twitter: **@ATCLondon**
FB: **www.facebook.com/ actorstouringcompany**
Insta: **actorstouringcompanyatc**

 Theatre
Royal
Plymouth

Theatre Royal Plymouth is a registered charity providing art, education and community engagement throughout Plymouth and the wider region. We engage and inspire many communities through performing arts and we aim to touch the lives and interests of people from all backgrounds. We do this by creating and presenting a breadth of shows on a range of scales, with our extensive creative engagement programmes, by embracing the vitality of new talent and supporting emerging and established artists, and by collaborating with a range of partners to provide dynamic cultural leadership for the city of Plymouth.

Recent productions and co-productions include *God Of Chaos*, by Phil Porter, *The Kneebone Cadillac* by Carl Grose, *You Stupid Darkness! by Sam Steiner* (with Paines Plough) and *The Unreturning* by Anna Jordan (with Frantic Assembly).

Producer Louise Schumann
Artistic Associate David Prescott
Production Manager Hugh Borthwick

Follow @TRPlymouth on Twitter
Follow @theatreroyalplymouth on Instagram
Like Theatre Royal Plymouth on Facebook

theatreroyal.com

Registered Charity No. 284545

AMSTERDAM

Maya Arad Yasur

Note on Play

The play is intended for a minimum of three performers.

The footnotes are to be read as onstage text, upon appearance in the book.

Acknowledgements

With special thanks to theatre director and dramaturg
Lilach Dekel-Avneri.

M.A.Y.

→ NON-
NATURALISTIC

ENSEMBLE - 4 actors.

PART ONE → · Mic in one corner.
· chair in another.
· Table + Bell + Typewriter
1. in another

– She, umm... what do they call it? She uh...

– Took a bite out of Amsterdam.

– Took a bite out of Amsterdam. Right; like it was some sort of omelette –

– She took a nice, juicy bite out of Amsterdam, right; like it was some sort of omelette she'd made without even cracking her eggs.

– She couldn't crack her eggs.

– She couldn't crack her eggs. Okay; what, like in a glass-ceiling kind of way?

– No. She couldn't crack her eggs. There was no glass ceiling. Hell, there wasn't even any ceiling there. Just eggs. A pair of them she literally had in her hands but couldn't crack to make the omelette or pancake or whatever it was she was trying to make. Yes.

– So she didn't crack the eggs.

– She didn't crack the eggs, no, she just let them run in her hands, or maybe she just put them back in the fridge or whatever, cos what was it, the gas was turned off?

– The gas was turned off. That's it. The gas had been turned off cos –

– Well here's the thing; she has no idea why.

– Her gas had been turned off and she has no idea why.

– No idea why. Truth is, she's no idea why her gas should have been turned off, until all of sudden –

STORY WAS UNEVEN.

→ vague to start
   off with

2.

–   8.27 a.m. And all of a sudden – a knock at the door.

–   The postman.

–   No, the postman never takes the stairs.

–   Not ever?

–   Not ever. In Amsterdam, the postman never takes the stairs.
    In Amsterdam, the postman pops the envelopes through that
    flap thingy in the front door that's facing the street –

–   Flap thingy; right.

–   He just pops them through and then they start piling up on
    the stairs in bulk.

–   The residents get in the stairwell, and because they'd like
    to avoid having to step on a pile of envelopes, they take
    their time digging out the ones that are addressed to them
    and the rest – yeah well, the rest, they put together in a
    perfectly neat pile and leave it on the second step. Could
    be the third step too, though.

–   Fourth step – at most.

–   And this postman, Hendri he's called; yes, Hendri, he's
    not your garden-variety postman, oh no! He isn't some Joe
    Schmo cycling around town in the dark, delivering people
    their letters just to make ends meet.

–   He's not?

–   No, man's a biomedical engineering student.

–   But the postman's not very crucial here, is he? No one's
    really all that interested in hearing about the postman; not
    really. The postman could be a biomedical engineering
    student; he could also be some street tramp for that matter;
    a rock star, refugee… hell, he could even be one of the
    Royals. Point is, the postman's just the footnote, cos the
    only thing we really care about are the envelopes. Those
    envelopes that he pops through those front door flap
    thingies, day-in, day-out.

– That's how it's done in Amsterdam. And they all do it the same way.

– And Victoria always gets them stuck in her heels.

who the story is about

– Merde!

– We'll have to come back to Victoria a little later. Because, right now, we have –

– A knock at the door.

– But they don't knock on doors in Amsterdam.

– Except there very much is a knock at the door right now. And there is no way it could be anyone else, anyone but the upstairs neighbour, cos it's a small building; only two storeys; and each one's only got the one flat.

– Only the one flat, that's right. And no one, no one but her and the upstairs neighbour has the key to the front door that's facing the street.

– Well it must be the neighbour, then. Must be the neighbour, the one called Jan.

– Must be the old, upstairs neighbour called Jan who's always smoking those cigars that stink up the stairwell.

– The narrow, winding stairwell, with the old, red carpet.

– The old red carpet that's soaked in Jan's stinking cigar smell.

MYSTERIOUS

– Jan? Jan, is that you?

– She answers the door and sees –

– No one.

– No one?

– No one. Just an envelope that Jan – yeah, must have been Jan – that he'd slid under her door. That's it. Slid it right under her door.

– Slid her an envelope right under the door and then just walked away.

–   Unless he didn't knock on the door.

–   But there was a knock at the door.

–   Because he doesn't want her seeing him.

–   He did knock on the door.

–   He doesn't want her smelling old age on him.

–   He doesn't want her smelling all that cheese on him.

–   But he did knock on the door.

–   They don't knock on doors in Amsterdam.

–   He won't knock on the door because he doesn't want her –

–   But he did knock on the door!

–   They don't bloody knock on doors in Amsterdam!

–   Smelling those cigars on him.

–   That's not it.

–   The jenever then.

–   That's not it!

–   The smell of those cigars he'd picked up at the tobacconist's on Damrak.

–   No, that's not it…

–   The smell of the jenever he always buys at the Wynand Fockink distillery under the Krasnapolsky Hotel at Dam.

–   No!

–   Dam Square, yes, the one she always cycles through on her way to Frascati Theatre.

–   Dam Square, the one she always cycles through on her way home from Central Station.

–   When she's getting the train back from Rotterdam after a concert.

–   Yes!

–   When she's getting the train back from Maastricht after rehearsal.

–   Yes!

–   When she's getting the train back from Utrecht after rehearsal.

–   Yes!

–   When she's getting the train back from Paris.

–   Yes!

–   When she's getting the train back from Berlin.

–   Yes!

–   When she's catching a plane back from Tel Aviv and heading to Central Station – by train.

–   But Jan doesn't. He doesn't go to Central Station.

–   Jan only pops over to Dam every six months when he's run out of jenever.

–   Wynand Fockink, superior jenever –

–   One-hundred-per-cent distilled juniper.

–   He cycles from his road and all the way to Dam Square; into an alleyway right under the Krasnapolsky, locks the bike to itself, props it up against the amsterdammertje[1] and heads into the distillery.

–   Hans is there to welcome him.

–   Hans?

–   Uh-huh, Hans. Good old smiley, bald-headed, Amsterdammer Hans –

–   Bald-headed, Amsterdammer Hans who looks like a yellow, life-size, smiling emoji; like the most perfect hunk of aged Dutch Gouda; like radiant sunshine at high noon, who goes up to him and says:

---

1. A small, short post at the edge of the pavement

–   Dag Meneer Jan, wat kan ik voor U doen?[2]

–   Like he doesn't know Jan's there for his fresh bottle of jenever.

–   Like he doesn't know Jan shows up once every six months like clockwork when he's run out of jenever.

–   Thirty years now!

–   Forty!

–   Fifty!

–   Like he doesn't know Jan's about to ask him for a fresh bottle of Jenever Superior to take away.

–   Not before he's had one for the road; and then has himself a little go at some random German tourist, telling them to 'Give me back my bicycle!'

–   While having a bit of a laugh under his moustache.

–   Bit of a laugh?

–   Under his moustache.

–   His bicycle.

–   The bicycles that the Germans took from the Dutch.

–   Huh?

–   In World War II.

–   Not before the German tries to cool off his flushed cheeks.

–   And Jan half-mutters something about how 'they took all our bikes, all of them'.

–   Huh?

–   For the iron.

–   He, uh... he wouldn't knock on her door.

–   He wouldn't knock on her door cos he doesn't want to have to look at her.

---

2. Hello Mr Jan, sir, what can I do for you?

– Her noxious, Sachsenhausen, schlimazel, Yiddish schnorrerising shtetl face coming at him.

– Who, Jan?

– Her noxious, Sachsenhausen shtetl face, and that dark, unruly mop of hair.

– Bit like Anne Frank's, eh?

– Those Jewish eyes plotting to take over the world.

– Her Jewish gaze, usurping his view.

– Her Jewish breath, stinking up his air.

– Those filthy tassels she's got the kid in her belly wearing; right there in her womb.

– Who, Jan? Nah…

– Jan, that's right. Jan.

– The upstairs neighbour?

– No, surely not. Not Jan.

– Then. Why. In. Fuck's. Name. Won't. He. Knock. On. That. Door –

– He doesn't want to inconvenience her. He doesn't want to inconvenience her because he knows she's nine months pregnant.

– But the envelope.

– Yes, the envelope. The khaki envelope from Israel.

– No.

– The envelope from Israel with the uh –

– No.

– The envelope from the, what was it, the Amsterdam Conservatory?

– No.

–   The Brussels Philharmonic.

–   No.

–   Carnegie Hall!

–   No.

–   What, an envelope with the Amsterdam coat of arms?[3]

–   Yup, that's the one.

–   Hebrew: Schelet Ha'azulah schel Amsterdam –

–   Nederlands: Het wapen van Amsterdam –

–   Polski: Herb Amsterdamu –

–   Español: El escudo de Amsterdam –

–   Dansk: Amsterdams byvåben –

–   Valiant, steadfast, compassionate.[4]

–   'Never shall I forget the emotion that overwhelmed us
      when eyewitnesses first notified us in London of how the
      entire population had actually turned against the
      inhumanity of the cruel tyrant.[5]'

–   So, Jan eh?

–   Jan; that's right. Jan.

–   Must have been something urgent.

–   So urgent he couldn't just leave it on one of those
      red-carpeted stairs?

---

3. The Amsterdam coat of arms is the official city symbol, and is made up of a
red shield and a black pale, with three silver St Andrew's cross, the imperial
crown of Austria, and two golden lions. The words 'valiant,' 'steadfast' and
'compassionate' are imprinted at the bottom.
4. During the 1941 February strike in Amsterdam, for the first time in Europe,
non-Jewish people protested against the persecution of Jews by the Nazi
regime. Queen Wilhelmina of the Netherlands wanted to commemorate the role
of the residents of Amsterdam during World War II and coined the following
three-word motto: 'Valiant, Steadfast, Compassionate'. On March 29 1947,
Wilhelmina presented the motto as part of the coat of arms of Amsterdam to the
city government. Her words were:
5. The Queen's words. To be delivered in a stately, regal tone.

– So urgent he just had to drag his pair of withered old legs up two storeys, slide it under her door and knock?

– They don't knock on doors in Amsterdam!

– It's a letter from the council, it's a –

– Bill.

– A bill. Right. Okay. A bill. For –

– Gas – *[handwritten: → play on the use of gas for the holocaust.]*

– A gas bill so urgent it adds up to –

– Seventeen hundred euros.

– Seventeen hundred eu…?

– Tssss…

– Euros?!

– For gas?!

– What'd she do, start her own scuba-tank top-up station?

– Send a hybrid rocket into space?

– Exterminate an entire people?

– Pause. *[handwritten: → letting the audience take in the extremity]*

– Pause?

– What d'you have to go and call 'pause' for?!

– You brought up genocide.

– So?

– You gotta have a pause after genocide.

– Come again?

– A pause.   *[handwritten: → QUESTIONING]*

– You mean after *the word* 'genocide'.

– After the word 'genocide' – you have a pause.

– And another pause.

– 'Fermata', they call it in music. Fermata.

– Why music?

– Cos she's a violinist.

– She's a violinist?! *→ INCONSISTANT?*
                       NOT IN ORDER

– She's a violinist. That is correct. We'd neglected to mention that she is a violinist. And a rather successful one at that. She uh, she's the one who composed that famous concerto, what's it called…

– A violin concerto in A-minor.

– *The Starling Paradox*.

– A paradox?

– The starling's. She'd composed this concerto called *The Starling Paradox* and it, um… that concerto was the thing that brought her all her fame.

– Not fame; recognition. It only brought her recognition. Strictly on a local scale at this stage, with the odd mention here and there in some random, nearby European capital.

– Right, fermata it is.

– I suppose.

– We pause.

– An indefinite pause.

– I suppose.

– Indefinite but not too long though.

– Just enough time to let the performer catch their breath.

– Exactly, or get in a quick rest.

– A rest, yes; but only the real quick one.

– It's only fair. Everyone would need one; they sure would –

–   When they've said the word –

–   Genocide.

PAUSE

3.   *movement around the stage as if in a queue.*

–   9.13 a.m.

–   She's at the supermarket. Queuing at the till. Some white guy right behind her; this bored look in his eyes.

–   Critical.

–   Critical, right. Judgemental. Cos he's probably thinking she's an immigrant.

–   He's sizing up the shopping in her basket.

–   A packet of spaghetti; bottle of French wine; bag of Brussels sprouts and some pastrami.

–   He could also be thinking she's Italian.

–   Except he doesn't, does he? The only thing he can think of is how she's taking up his place in the queue.

–   She's thinking he's thinking about how she's taking up his place in the queue.

–   That if she weren't there, then the supermarket queues would be that much shorter.

–   Queues in the post office would be that much shorter.

–   The pharmacy too.

–   That if she weren't there, then he might have been the one living in her Keizersgracht flat. He'd always wanted to live on the Keizersgracht.[6] She's gone and hijacked his Keizersgracht flat.

---

6. The Emperor's Canal – the second and widest of the four canals in Amsterdam's city centre.

–   Cos she also wants to live on the Keizersgracht. She also
    wants to stand on her parquet floors in her sloffen,[7] press
    her thighs up against the central heating and look out the
    double-glazed window at the ducks in the canal; she also
    wants to be looking down at her bicycle that she keeps tied
    up to this little bridge with two chains; and her grocery
    bag she's left lying on the rack like some saddle for drunks
    to dump empty Heineken cans inside.

–   Or piss a can's worth of Heineken into.

–   He thinks she's religious. He's noticed it's pastrami she's
    buying and not ham, and now he's convinced she's
    religious. That she's this Orthodox Muslim.

–   So?

–   And he's seen her grab the pastrami from the shelf that
    says 'Halal'[8] in Dutch and in Arabic and now he thinks
    she's Muslim.

–   So?

–   So he thinks she's Muslim.

–   He thinks she's Muslim and as such, he's thinking that
    she's taking up his place in the queue.

–   He's thinking she's taking up two places in the queue.

–   He's thinking I've got this parasite in my belly that's
    going to feed off *his* faxes! she's thinking.

–   His faxes? What the hell's she on about?

–   Taxes. His taxes.

–   Just tell him you're Jewish. He could be a Jew himself,
    she tells herself.

–   Tell him you're from Israel. He might be –

–   She's got that gas bill in her hand. The one she got in the
    post –

–   From Jan.

---

7. Slippers.
8. The Arab word for the Muslim equivalent of Kosher food.

–   She's got that gas bill in her hand that she got from Jan.

–   Ask him if he could translate for you. Speak English but use your American accent, she's telling herself. Let him know that you've got a master's, she's telling herself; that you're this woman of the world, that you're from a Western country –

– Ha!

– A secular country –

– Haha!

– A democracy –

– Ha! Ha! HA!

– Let him know that you're a violinist. That you're Jewish.

– She's thinking that he's thinking the cashier's a dead ringer for her. She's thinking that he's thinking how underneath that hijab is a girl who's the spitting image of her. That they've both got the same complexion and the same eyes. He's thinking she's this secular Muslim, Moroccan or Turkish maybe. That she must work as a cashier for some other supermarket chain.

– Even cashiers have to go to the supermarket for their shopping.

– So she's wearing her headphones. She's singing in English.

– She's thinking he's going to think she's Italian.

– He's thinking she's either this Italian who's picking up some French wine or some secular Muslim cashier who's feeding off his –

– She's asking the cashier for the total; in English.

– Why English?! Dutch! Speak Dutch!

– Now's not the time to be practising her Dutch.

– Ik moet mijn Nederlands oefenen[9] –

9. I should be practising my Dutch.

- What's she going on about?

- Ik moet mijn klote Nederlands oefenen[10] –

- Accent alert!

- She's only speaking English to the cashier.

- She's saying she doesn't speak Dutch; wants them to think she's a tourist; an American. She's tickling their every prejudice; exercising their every stereotyping muscle; she's shuffling their every nationalist card. She's telling herself –

- Be political.

- Heil Hitler!

- Be socially conscious.

- Viva la revolución!

- Be one of us.

- Immigrants go home!

- Be who you are.

- Europe for Europeans!

- Be practical!

- Twee halen een betalen![11]

- Show him the gas bill you got from Jan today.

- Tsssss…

- Remind him where he comes from with his local craft beer and those bacon rashers he's got in his basket.

- Hamas, Hamas, joden aan het gas[12] –

- Tell him!

- Mevrouw?[13]

- A seventeen-hundred-euro gas bill, in the name of van Heugten –

---

10. I should be practising my fucking Dutch.
11. Take two, pay for the one.
12. Hamas, Hamas, Jews to the gas.
13. Miss?

–   Mevrouw.

–   Mevrouw van Heugten?

–   The landlady. May she rest.

–   Mevrouw!

–   Mevrouw van Heugten –

–   Mevrouw!!!!

–   JA?

–   Jij bent aan de beurt.[14]

–   Tsssss…

–   Halal pastrami, loaf of spelt bread, some mayonnaise, and a gherkin.

–   Seventeen hundred euros.

–   Mag ik contant betalen?[15]

4.

–   11.25 a.m. she's having a –

–   Transvaginal ultrasound examination.

–   Transvaginal ultrasound examination, right. And there's a pulse, is there?

–   Pause.

–   Is there a pulse?   — USE OF THE
                                        MIC AS HEART
                                              BEAT

–   Pause.

–   She's asking to listen for a pulse.

–   Pause.

---

14. You're next.
15. Could I pay cash?

–   She wants to tell the doctor she's a violinist.

–   She wants to tell him she used to play with the Amsterdam Philharmonic.

–   I bet he goes to concerts.

–   I bet his father goes to concerts.

–   I bet his father goes to concerts and the opera.

–   I bet he listens to Wagner when he's making dinner, conducting the pots and frying pans with all his ladles and spoons.

–   And turning up the flame on the gas hob, muttering in German: 'gesamtkunstwerk'.

–   Gesamtkunstwerk.

–   She thinks it might be wise to share something personal with him –

–   Just as he's sticking that contraption between her legs?

–   Share something personal like –

–   Living? Dead?

–   Something about herself. About her Dutchman. Help him relate to her while he's having all his anti-Semitic thoughts about her jet-black pubes.

–   Share something. Anything.

–   Something about that party back in Belgium. At that sixteenth-century castle, in Spontin.

–   Skull circumference: thirty-two centimetres.

–   Right, in Spontin. At that castle. At the servants' wing.

–   Weight estimation: two kilos, seven hundred grams.

–   She took Methylenedioxymethamphetamine.

–   Took what now?

–   Ecstasy. E. She took some E and she touched the stars. Just before midnight. The very last ten seconds, during the

(margin, handwritten, vertical) SELF CONCIOUSNESS

actual countdown. Oh yeah, right, because it was New Year's Eve and there were fireworks outside the castle, in the snow, and she went outside; she went outside, even though her dress; the dress she had bought especially for that party in Spontin at some tiny vintage shop on one of the Jordaan's nine streets; that mustard-coloured dress with the red zigzag pattern, had no sleeves.

– Five toes on the right foot.

– And her Dutchman told her off: you have to have a coat on! He was saying, either get back in the castle or go put on a coat!

– External auditory meatus.

– He said, let's make love by the fireplace.

– She's telling him how her Dutchman said to her, 'Let's make love by the fireplace,' except he's not even listening because he's busy; uh-huh, yes, he's busy assessing her baby's body with his ultrasound stick that he's shoved right between her thighs.

– He's looking her in the eye, seeing pink nipples.

– He's looking her in the eye, seeing the nipples of naked Jewish women running through the ghetto, and he can't say whether he wants to shoot her, or fuck her, or save her, then marry her.

– He sees in her a Jew with flashing euro signs in her eyes like they do in the cartoons. He's looking her in the eye, seeing her breasts. He's looking her in the eye, seeing Christ walk on water. He's looking her in the eye, seeing nothing but a nose. He's thinking:

– She hasn't got a Jewish nose.

– Actually.

– Huh?

– Actually.

- She hasn't got a Jewish nose. Actually.

- She's thinking that if she tells him she lives on the Keizersgracht then he won't think –

- Mm-hmm?

- That she's some piss-poor immigrant living at some neighbourhood no one has the guts to set foot in –

- Not even the police.

- That if she tells him she lives on the Keizersgracht right by the Photography Museum.

- That if he knew she was here because she wanted to be.

- That if he knew she was here because she could be.

- That if he knew she was here because her whole life's an adventure.

- That if she told him about her Keizersgracht flat.

- That if she told him about the nooks in the walls.

- She doesn't know yet about the nooks in the walls.

- That if she told him about the nooks and the burrows.

- That if she told him about the gas bill.

- That's it! Bingo. That is exactly what she needs to do. She needs to tell him about the gas bill.

- She knows she needs to tell him about the gas bill. She knows she wants to show him that gas bill and have him explain what it says and how she's ended up with that bill. Why she, of all people, should end up getting such a crazy-high gas bill; and if she has got a seventeen-hundred-euro gas leak on her hands then how is she not dead yet? She knows he can translate for her, but instead, she just starts going on about her flat on the Keizersgracht; the canal-facing window; the chopped tree that's got baby shoes hanging from it, and instead of telling him just how much she adores that view from that window; instead of telling him how incredibly fortunate she feels, having found a flat on the Keizersgracht; instead, she comes out with –

– These views don't look anything like the landscapes of my childhood.

– Thump-thump-thump-thump…

– Pulse is dropping.

– Is the fetus in distress?

– Pulse is dropping.

– She could also tell him she wrote *The Starling Paradox*.

– Represented the Netherlands with pride!

– Ben ik van Duitsen bloed!!![16]

– Will the audience please rise –

– Ben ik van Duitsen bloed!!!

– When we were kids, every Saturday, we'd drive to Michmoret Beach, and on our way back, in the evening, just as it was starting to get dark, we would see all the flocks of starlings through the car window.

– He'd like to gift her his childhood landscapes.

– Starlings all fly in unison in the same direction and then, all at once – in pitch-perfect synchronicity, they'll change direction. And it's not as if they do that to entertain the humans. Oh no. It's not some perfectly timed, flawlessly choreographed performance delivered by transient guests; no sir; because this is not the theatre! And we are not their audience. Oh no, no, no, no, they don't know we're watching, and not only do they not realise we're watching, the fact is, they couldn't care less about any one of us.

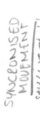
SYNCHRONISED MOVEMENT / stylised

– Mm-hmm?

– It's how they defend themselves.

---

16. Dutch for 'I am of German bloodline.' A line from the Dutch national anthem. When asked to sing the national anthem, she rewrites the lyrics to say 'Ben ik van Joodse bloed', i.e. 'I am of Jewish bloodline.'

–   Ah...

–   In a blink of an eye, the flock which not two seconds ago
    was this tightest, roundest mass cutting across the sky; it
    opens wide, creating this backdraft that flicks the predator
    right on its back.

–   Pow!

–   When he hears she's from Israel, he smiles a right wicked
    smile.

–   He loves her militant streak.

–   For God's sake, she's a violinist!

–   Could be the army, or the kibbutz, or this collective sense
    of paranoia –

–   He's fantasising about her out in the desert, M16 in her
    hand.

–   Israelis have got a bit of a starling mentality, haven't they?

–   That word, 'starling', it's that word.

–   Right, because in Amsterdam, she could be the starling she
    is without having to follow the flock's rules, timing or
    direction.

–   She, herself, is a bit of paradox that needs resolving.

–   Uh-uh. It's not a paradox. It's a polyphony is what it is –
    every voice is its own independent, rhythmic entity with
    no voice playing second fiddle.

–   She is a violinist.

–   She is a paradox. She is *The Starling Paradox*.

–   Tell him how Jan slipped the envelope under your door.
    Tell him you opened that letter and found that gas bill.
    Ask him to translate; explain it to you; tell you what to do.

–   He's having a peek inside her vagina, thinking to himself:
    So this is what a Jewish cunt looks like.

–   He's having a sniff at her vagina, thinking to himself: So this is what a Jewish cunt smells like.

–   She's showing him the bill, saying, yes, she's saying:

–   Look –

–   Gas.

–   Bill.

–   A thousand-seven-hundred euros.

–   Tssssss…

–   We got a pulse.

–   Thump-thump-thump –

–   Tsssss…

–   Thump-thump-thump –

–   Tsssss…

–   Thump-thump-thump –

5.

–   Half one in the afternoon. She is sat in front of her agent. Her agent, yeah, who's in charge of representing the most promising talent to have come out of Europe's conservatories in recent years. She's sat in front of her, thinking:

–   Hang on; is she seriously asking me this? Are you seriously asking me this?

–   She is seriously asking her this; looking her dead straight in the eye and asking without even flinching:

–   Yeah.

–   Mm-hmm?

–   She's asking her the question that's rendered her frozen; as if
     it was January again and the council was still busy picking
     the last remaining shards of broken champagne bottles left
     over from New Year's on the side of the road in the snow.

–   She's asking her a question that's rendered her tongue
     paralysed; as if everyone, all at once forgot they ever
     spoke English and are making her – yes, literally making
     her, that is if she'd like to be understood – Making her say
     it all in Dutch; no mistakes and not a hint of an accent.

–   She's asking her the question that –

–   Why don't you compose a requiem for five hundred and
     fifty-one dead children?

–   Excuse me?

–   In Gaza. That's what she's asking her: Why don't you
     compose a requiem for five hundred and fifty-one dead
     children in Gaza?

–   Why should she compose a requiem for five hundred and
     fifty-one dead children?

–   Because they like it political is why. They'll think she's all
     'woke', yeah? A proper Westerner; that there are others
     like her in that slaughterhouse she comes from; fancy her
     a beacon of light in the great darkness, won't they? While
     everyone knows, all of them, herself included; even she
     knows that when all's said and done, she is no more than
     a fig leaf hiding the thing everyone else would be that
     much happier never having to look at.

–   Why should I have to carry this giant flag around with me,
     everywhere I go? She's asking.

–   She's asking; even though she knows too well what the
     answer is. She knows that at the end of the day, she is nine
     months pregnant, and that even though it is recommended
     that during this ninth month, one doesn't lift or carry any
     heavy loads, say like a flag – this final, ultimate month
     symbolises that at last, after all these years, she's finally

going to have a child. And that is not to say; oh no, in no way, shape or form is that to say that even if there are five hundred and fifty-one dead children; that even if one woman across the border has had three of her children die on her after a two hundred and fifty kilogram bomb fell right next door to them; none of that's to say that she isn't allowed her own baby –

– And after all, it's not as if she has to write a requiem for five hundred and fifty-one dead children.

– She; who barely even had a mother and father herself and who's only ever wanted a small family to call her own;

– She; who has seen everyone else pretty much give up on the prospect of her ever having children.

– She of all people; but they don't care about that, do they? No, sir; when's she's off scoring a concerto about love, or painting still life, or writing a story about some girl from whatever country.

– Why do they keep smearing me with all this blood? She wonders.

– She wonders because she is also a human being; and she is also a woman; and she also gets a little damp between her legs when a strange man's lips brush against her ear on a plane, asking if he could possibly get through.

– Huh?

– Because after all, she hasn't killed anyone, has she?

– Because it's true; and it would be highly unfair to argue otherwise. That she didn't push that button.

– And it's true that it's nobody's damn business, who she voted for in the general election.

– And that she doesn't have to answer to anyone about her reasons for serving in the army.

– Why she would put on a uniform –

– What size –

–   Why she would salute some pot-bellied, bearded man with all his ranks on –

–   Stupid bitch –

–   Why she fucked those senior officers while they were waiting on updates from the field as this swarm of planes made in one country, dropped bombs made in another country on the buildings of a third country.

–   Why she would sing the national anthem –

–   With pride, no less –

–   And keep her chin up with conviction, in a convergent harmony of rising chins, male phalluses and flags flying at full mast.

–   That's her chin.

–   And her vagina.

–   And her teeth.

–   And her finger.

–   And that baby, it's hers.

–   And it would have EU citizenship!

–   Yes it will!

–   Because it came into the world in Europe. One might say, it came into Europe.

–   And those are the rules!

–   Ha!

–   The rules…

–   (You do so love your rules!)

–   And its father dumped his Aryan sperm inside her; with his one-point-ninety metres of pure muscle, high IQ and blue-eyed promises of genetic supremacy; complemented by an affinity for bureaucracy and genocide.

–   Pause!

–   Fermata –

–   I suppose –

–   We pause.

–   But why won't she talk to her about her music?

–   About *The Starling Paradox* –

–   So instead of talking to her about *The Starling Paradox*;
     instead of talking to her about her music; instead of telling
     her it is none of her goddamn business whether she does or
     does not compose a requiem for five hundred and fifty-one
     dead or not-so-dead children; instead –

–   Instead, she gets the bill out; that bill she couldn't pluck
     up the courage to show that guy at the supermarket, or the
     doctor who had stuck that soundwavey rod thing between
     her thighs; that bill she's been schlepping round in her bag
     all day; that her neighbour, Jan had slipped under her door.
     That seventeen-hundred-euro gas bill; that's what she gets
     out to show her agent from her contemporary classical
     music record label.

6.

–   She does love the clicking of her heels along the
     Keizersgracht pavement.

–   Especially when she takes the rubbish out.

–   At night.

–   The night before collection day.

–   Four bin liners in hand –

–   Paper here; glass over here; plastic over there.

–   Selection!

–   Pause.

–   Why pause?

–   When she's wearing those shoes with the small, wooden heels –

–   Those echoing shoes –

–   You gotta lay off the booze!

–   The echoing of Herman Brood's heels –

–   That's it!

–   When he comes out of his van and goes into the Paradiso; through the artists' entrance –

–   Echoing in her heels!

–   Yes!

–   The echoing of –

–   Gerrit Rietveld's heels!

–   Yes!

–   Clicking against the concert-hall sidewalk as he's brainstorming his plans for the Van Gogh Museum building –

–   Echoing in her heels!

–   Yes!

–   Spinoza's heels!

–   Yes!

–   Otto –

–   Yes!

–   Huh?! Otto Frank's heels –

–   Yes!

–   Over on 263 Prinsengracht

–   Echoing in her heels.

–   Yes!

– Oberscharführer SS Karl Silberbauer's[17] heels

– Yes!

– Echoing in her heels.

– Yes!

– How they echo-cho-cho-cho-cho-cho-cho... those shoes –

– Whose echo cuts through the envelope in the bag; the letter inside the envelope in the bag; the number on the letter inside the envelope in the bag.

– Yes!

– The echo in her shoes...

– Oh yes!

– Of 'Death to the Jews' –

– Yes!

– Echoing in her heels.

7.

– 8.07 in the evening. She's circling a glass of red wine with those violinist fingers of hers and having a conversation with, who's she talking to, the guy or the girl behind the bar, or is it the –

– She's got that friend; Victoria.

– That Victoria she met in Dutch class?

– That Victoria she met in Dutch class who then dragged her all the way across town to this place in the east where everyone was into freestyle storytelling; or that club over at the Overtoorn where they're always showing the old Hollywood classics down in the basement.

17. The SD officer who was head of the squad that had stormed the Franks' hideout on 263 Prinsengracht.

- All the foreigners hang out there.

- All the foreigners hang out there cos that's the only place; yeah, that's right, that is the only place, among all the outcasts that they feel themselves part of some caste.

- Victoria was born in Belgrade. Or was it Sofia? Or Stockholm?

- Born in Belgrade, right, but studied in Madrid.

- Studied in Madrid, right, but then emigrated to Milan.

- Emigrated to Milan, right, but trained in India.

- Set up shop in Amsterdam, right, because she fell in love with that Nigel fella, who was actually Irish.

- She takes her show all over the world.

- That feminist show of hers, right, with that big old skirt that sprawls out like the sea.

- But not like the wavy if not stormy sea when it brushes against Seagull Island on Tantura Beach.

- Nah, more like the high waves that slam into the Black Sea coastline when Victoria is doing all that spinning in front of an audience.

- When Victoria is on her bike, cycling through the streets of Calvinist Amsterdam.

- Yes!

- In her Russian fur hat!

- Or in her fishnet stockings under her short shorts.

- Yes!

- No inhibitions whatsoever, that one, eh?!

- No inhibitions whatsoever and also, doesn't give a fuck what anyone thinks of her.

- She trains with Soviet-like devotion.

- Spinning round and round the world –

–   Oh yeah!

–   She's a hyper-feminist, she is.

–   Oh yeah!

–   Her hyper-feminism is verging on man-hating.

–   Man-hating, oh yeah, and yet –

–   And yet?

–   And yet, sometimes she has to do the odd belly-dancing stint at some Lebanese restaurant –

–   Belly-dancing; right, to make ends meet.

–   And does she get up in arms about Muslim women and their burkas or what?

–   She's packing some pretty xenophobic-sounding opinions –

–   She's packing some pretty misogynistic-sounding opinions –

–   She's packing some pretty Islamophobic-sounding opinions –

–   Cos she's got privilege.

–   Cos she's a woman.

–   Cos she's a foreigner.

–   Cos she's half-Muslim herself.

–   Cos she's a refugee.

–   So Victoria; that same Victoria; she's asking her, what's with the envelope?

–   She grabs the envelope, yeah? Asking her, 'What is this bill?'

–   She's asking what the number means.

–   She hands it over to the bartender; get him to translate for her.

–   She hands it over the hot, Dutch bartender at the Stanislavski to translate for her.

–   She's telling the hot, Dutch bartender at the Stanislavski: she's too embarrassed to ask, herself.

–   That she feels way too embarrassed to ask, herself, and that she's been carrying this bill around with her all day.

–   Even though she has shown that bill; she absolutely has shown that bill to that agent of hers from the contemporary classical music record label; and that agent; the same agent who'd suggested she write a requiem for five hundred and fifty-one dead children could only shrug her shoulders and half-mutter a 'ik heb geen flauw idée'.[18]

–   Victoria sniggers and starts telling him about India.

–   He's got the gas bill in his hands, trying to figure it out except he can't, can he? Because he's got Victoria with her tonic water right there in front of him banging on and on…

–   Cos Victoria's telling him about Madrid –

–   Cos Victoria's telling him about Milan –

–   Cos Victoria's telling him about Belgrade –

–   About the war –

–   About that Bosnian fella her father was hiding in their home.

–   About that Bosnian fella her father was hiding in their home who would touch her at night.

–   About her father who'd kicked her out for trash-talking that Bosnian soldier.

–   Until finally –

–   Yes, finally; at last, Victoria pauses. She comes up for merciful air.

–   That's right. She's taken a pause; a 'pausette', rather. And it is during her 'pausette' that the bartender says, 'Your landlord's not paid her bill.'

---

18. I haven't the foggiest idea.

- He's saying, 'This is a bill from 1944.'

- And mumbling something about how 'this sum total also includes fines and arrears interest.'

- And asking, '289 Keizersgracht, is that your address?'

- That is in fact her address.

- 'I could try and do some digging for you,' he tells her. Cos he's got this brother-in-law or neighbour, or childhood friend or whatever…

- His squash partner!

- His squash partner! Ooh, that's a good one. He works at the council archives.

- And he writes down her address, '289 Keizersgracht' on a beer coaster; and he writes down her landlady's name on top of the address, 'Ingrid van Heugten'; and the beer coaster, he folds up twice, then stuffs inside his coat pocket. That's right, the barman. And he promises he'll see what he can do.

- And then, Victoria starts telling him about this shelved Antonioni movie she was in as an extra, in some Italian whorehouse scene, and Antonioni let her keep the corset.

- She's telling him about that time she sat nude for Jean-Pierre Pelletier and how he had a massive hard-on in his baggies the whole time.

- The way Jean-Pierre; yeah, Jean-Pierre she's calling him; the way he committed her breasts to canvas with broad, nostalgic brushstrokes and then sold them off for nine hundred thousand dollars in an auction at some upmarket New York City gallery.

- But Victoria, oh, Victoria, all that work and not a single shekel, dollar, euro or goddamn franc even to show for it!

- But she will be; rest assured. Oh yes, she will – that is by far the most important thing – that Victoria be forever enshrined.

8.

– If she moves back home, it wouldn't necessarily mean she'd end up busking on a stool at Dizengoff Square with her violin.

– Well no; there are other squares.

– If she moves back home, is there even a chance she'd be walking down the road and some rando would just come up to her and hand her a pile of classical music records?

– Yes!

– As a gift?

– No.

– Or that it would start raining?

– There is a chance. But only a slim one.

9.

– When she goes for a swim in Amsterdam's public swimming pool, she feels like an eleven-year-old again, standing in front of the mirror at the Galei Gil swimming pool in Ramat Gan, parting her hair with a comb. Her hair's all wet. It's nine degrees outside. 'I really could do with a warme chocolademelk',[19] she says.

– Goed zo![20]

– Dutch teacher loves you.

– Wat eten de mensen in jouw eigen land?[21]

– Hummus en kip op een stok.[22]

---

19. Hot chocolate.
20. Well done!
21. What do the people eat in your home country?
22. Hummus and skewered chicken.

– Goed zo!

– Dutch teacher loves you.

– And when she asked for a bob at the hairdresser's and the man said, 'Maar je hebt geen Europese haar'[23] –

– She loves walking along the Amstel to just sit there and watch that clunky, gargantuan bridge split in two as if it were the Red Sea, rising into the air like a pair of black monster pricks, just to let the one boat through below. She goes, 'If I had a piemel[24]'…

– Dutch teacher loves you.

– 'I'd be walking around all boned up with pride, being part of mankind.'

– How about Jan?

– Jan's not surprised. Jan says he knows.

– Jan's got the envelope with the bill in his hand, and he's telling her, 'Wacht hier even'[25] –

– Why won't he ask her in?

– 6 p.m.

– Why won't he offer her a cup of coffee?

– Eten's tijd![26]

– Glass of water?

– Cos he'll be right back; he's just popping into the next room and he'll be right back,

– Right, Jan's back; Jan's coming back and he's handing her a parcel.

– Jan's back and he's handing her this large parcel; this bunch of yellowing papers tied together in, what is that, unspooled ribbon?

---

23. But you don't have European hair.
24. Willy (cock).
25. Wait right here.
26. Dinnertime (a typical-sounding figure of speech).

- These come every few months, he says.

- What does?

- The letters. The envelopes, these bills he has in his hand. The ones tied together with some piece of unspooled ribbon he'd fetched from the next room.

- The landlady wouldn't pay these, he said.

- Nor would her daughter pay these.

- Nor would her granddaughter pay these.

- This dates back to 1944 and all these years, no one's been willing to settle the bill. No one, because no one can bring themselves to; morally that is; none of the parties involved possessed the sense of justice that would allow them to reach into their wallets or purses and just pay up –

- Because –

- Because she wasn't home in those months! Ingrid van Heugten was not at home during those months when the gas was being used. He whispers.

- Where was she?

- 'The bloody Riviera!' He snaps. 'Where do you think?!'

- Why's he shouting?

- Where d'you think she would be?!

- And he slams the door.

- Cos she wasn't in those months.

- Those wretched months back in '44

- Those dark months back in '44

- She was in the shaft.

- The shaft?

- The deep, dark shaft that was 1944.

- Pause.

- I didn't say 'genocide'.

- Pretty sure I did. I called 'genocide'. I absolutely did. She was there, the landlady, Mevrouw Ingrid van Heugten; she was down in that shaft, all those months… she was there; she nearly was no more.

- Where was she?

- She was there. She was there.

- She was there; that's where she was.

- There?

- She was there. She was no more.

- She was no more?

- She was nearly no more.

- She was there and was nearly no more.

- Ingrid van Heugten?

- Her landlady. She made it back.

- She came back from the shaft?

- Ingrid van Heugten, yes, she came back from the shaft and she wouldn't pay that bill.

- I'll just go ahead and pay it, she says, all of a sudden.

- You?!

- Well, yeah. It's pretty straightforward. It suddenly dawns on her. 'I'll just pay it and that'll be that.'

- And Jan says, 'You can't pay this.'

- Sure I can! I can pay this.

- And Jan replies, 'But why should *you* have to pay it?'

- And she says, 'I'll get my mum to pay it.'

- Why should your mother have to pay?

- I'll get my nan to pay it.

–   Why should your grandmother have to pay?

–   'I'll just pay it, yeah? I'm going to pay it, and that's that,'
     she tells him. And with that, we have ourselves a verdict.
     With that, she says, this debt will be settled once and for
     all. Enough already.

–   Over my dead body.

–   Over our six million dead bodies.

–   Pause.

–   Hang on.

–   Pause?

–   Well yeah, I call pause cos, cos if she wasn't there then –

–   Then who was using the gas?

PART TWO

1.

– It's horrifying, cos of the symbolism; cos it's gas. And you just keep on saying that word, 'gas; gas; gas' just to amp up the horror, but at end of the day, it's all red tape, really. Amsterdam's post-war city clerks were no anti-Semites; no more than this one is. It's not as if they all hated Mevrouw van Heugten. Quite the opposite – they saw her as an equal and as such, insisted that she too pay her bills like everyone else.

– Come again?

– It's what they call here 'ambtenaar mentaliteit'.

– Clerk mentality.

– Let them call it 'clerk' mentality.' I call it –

– 'The mentality that gave the Nazis free rein to just swoop right in and murder seventy-five per cent of the Netherlands' Jewish population.'

– She wasn't even a Jew.

– Who, Mevrouw van Heugten?

– Yes. She was. She was a Jew.

– She was not a Jew –

– Then how'd she end up in Auschwitz, then?

– van Heugten's not a Jewish name.

– She was sent to Auschwitz, she was a Jew.

– Pause!!!

– van Heugten? A Jew? Seriously?

–   van Heugten, yeah. Maiden name was Cohen or Marcus,
    or whatever but she married some Dutch Aryan fella;
    right; yeah; yeah, she married this Dutch Aryan fella
    named Meneer van Heugten.

–   No. Uh-uh.

–   What?

–   She wasn't a Jew.

2.

*4.55 p.m. cycling en route to a town hall meeting at
Waterlooplein.*

–   Right, right, okay…

–   Okay what?

–   So she was married to a Dutchman, this Meneer van
    Heugten who was, what did he do – account manager at
    some steel factory?

–   No, he wasn't an account manager. He was a lawyer
    representing Jews who'd had their homes confiscated in
    the war.

–   He was a lawyer; they had their homes taken away in the
    war; he represented them. He defended them in these big,
    public trials that never did go their way in the end.

–   Oh, and he also represented some members of the
    Resistance.

–   Members of the Resistance; quite. Back in the early days
    of the war, when there was still the appearance at least of
    a balanced justice system.

–   He was standing up for all those political, ethnic, fucked-up,
    cast-out minorities.

- Those who'd been purged –

- Who'd been fucked –

- Who'd been relegated to rat and subhuman status –

- The queers –

- The Jews –

- The cripples –

- The cripples and those with the skin conditions.

- Even married them.

- All of them?!

- Mevrouw Ingrid van Heugten, who needed him.

- Mevrouw Ingrid van Heugten whose name is on this gas bill.

- Mevrouw Ingrid van Heugten, may the good Lord rest her soul.

- She was disabled.

- She was not disabled.

- She was ill.

- Nope.

- Deformed.

- No.

- A schizophrenic –

- She was none of those things.

- She had this skin condition; these lesion-type things all over her skin, looked like leprosy –

- No!

- She was beautiful, and regal. He didn't just fall in love with her over nothing.

– She was beautiful, and regal, and strong, and she had a pair on her! Balls like a superhero's.

– Cojones![27]

– Palle![28]

– Gogan![29]

– Ballen –

– Huh?

– 'Ballen.' The word's 'ballen' in Dutch, like 'bitterballen'[30].

– Fine. But she was Jewish. She was a well-off, educated Jew in a prominent position...

– She was well-off, educated, and held a prominent position which she was stripped of the moment war broke out –

– Exactly.

– Except she wasn't a Jew.

– She *was* a Jew! That is why they sent her to Auschwitz! Because she was a Jew!

– She held a prominent position she was stripped of just when the war began, but she wasn't Jewish.

– And Auschwitz?

– Oh yeah, but that wasn't cos she was Jewish.

– It wasn't?

– No. No. No one wants to hear about the Jews any more. It's been rehashed; replayed; regurgitated. Jews are... how shall I put it...

– Jews are passé –

– Jews are, that's it! Jews are passé –

---

27. Spanish for 'balls'.
28. Italian for 'balls'.
29. Kurdish for 'balls'.
30. A meaty Dutch snack containing a mix of cow and veal mince, butter, parsley, a bit of salt, pepper...

–   And Auschwitz?

–   Auschwitz? Oh yeah, sure. But it wasn't cos she was Jewish.

–   She wasn't?

–   She was a gypsy.

–   She was not a gypsy –

–   A lesbian gypsy with Communist beliefs.

–   No. They took her to Auschwitz because she was a fighter!

–   She was a fighter; right. She fought with the Resistance.

–   She wasn't a Jew?

–   No. She joined the Resistance.

–   Did she now?

–   She did indeed. That's her story. In fact, she was a very dominant figure in the Resistance.

–   I see. Hiding dozens of them in that nook in the wall.

–   Other nooks too.

–   There were other nooks?

–   And burrows. Other nooks and burrows. Whole burrows inside those walls.

–   Burrows, I see, burrows, right.

–   But surely, there had to have been at least one Jew in one of those burrows in the walls.

–   Okay fine, so maybe there was the one Jew. Ten even. Hiding in burrows right here in the walls of your study.

–   In the walls of the room where you compose your music.

–   In the walls of the room where you practise your music –

–   In the walls of the room where you practise your fingering –

–   In the walls of the room where your Dutchman practised his fingering.

– In the walls of the room where you conceived that child of yours.

– In the walls of the room where you plan on having that child of yours.

– In the walls of the room where you dreamt up, that's right, dreamt up *The Starling Paradox*.

– That's right.

– In the walls of the room where you fancy yourself part of a long line of Europeans.

– A long line of violinists.

– Just more sophisticated.

– More informed.

– More cultured.

– Yes, more cultured than your 'high-society' Tel Avivian who likes to hold her red wine by the stem – the glass's stem, that is – a glass that may look like it's crystal – but isn't really – crystal, that is.

– In this room, the nook that's right here in this room; Jews hiding in the burrows both Mevrouw and Meneer van Heugten had dug out in the walls.

– And one Jewess in particular.

– Is that so?

– One Jewess. Yes. One Jewess in particular who's been hiding in the burrows. This one Jewess, what's she called –

– The one he fell in love with.

– Who, Meneer van Heugten?

– He's in love with her. Always kissing her whenever his wife, Mevrouw van Heugten goes off on covert Resistance operations.

– With a Jew? In hiding?

– Yes. Married to Ingrid van Heugten. A brave fighter with the Resistance.

– He values her.

– Idolises her!

– But his heart belongs to another. A Jewess.

– Whose name is, what is it, Bertien?

– Yes. Bertien. Jewish girl.

3.

5.25 p.m. An appointment at the town hall.

– In the aforementioned time period, Mevrouw Ingrid van Heugten was being held at the Auschwitz death camp. And someone else, who was not Jewish. Could be Dutch, or even German for that matter; a Nazi soldier perhaps, some Nazi bureaucrat even, was staying illegally in her flat, using her utilities – the electricity, and gas! The gas!

– The gas, I see.

– Whilst she was in Auschwitz, in the gas chambers!

– I am aware of that, miss.

– Well why the penalty then?

– Because the bill has yet to be settled!

– Sir, I am not paying this bill if Hitler himself comes knocking on my door.

– Miss, if we could please leave Hitler out of this and focus on the matter at hand.

– But this is the matter at hand! It absolutely is the matter at hand.

–   The council is well within its rights to expect full
    compensation for all outstanding bills and penalties to
    which it is entitled.

–   The council's what? Well within its rights, is it?

–   What I am saying is that whatever excuses one might
    come up with as a way of avoiding payment –

–   Excuses? Her own property was seized by the –

–   …Including the argument that one's own property was
    seized by the Nazis, are simply invalid. Bills and any
    subsequent penalties for failure to settle them on time,
    must be paid. Regardless of whether a third party had been
    occupying the property, legally or otherwise.

–   I think you might be missing the point here. Could be that
    you're too young and maybe you don't know your history
    all that well – Mevrouw van Heugten was in Auschwitz in
    those months. Ever hear of that place? Name sound
    familiar?

–   AAAAAUUUuuuschwitz!

–   Is she having a contraction?

–   AAAAAUUUuuuschwitz!

–   She's having a contraction!!!

–   She was on her way to the gas chambers. Someone else
    was staying in her flat using her –

–   Gas.

–   Tssss…

–   Someone's gotta pay.

–   Yes, but who?

–   It doesn't matter to me one way or the other, miss,
    whoever pays this bill, just as long as it is paid already.
    Too many years this has been dragging on, unsettled.

4.

*1.03 a.m. A dream in which a soldier is taking a shit under
a cherry tree.*

–   (*Soldier.*) Look Mum, I'm standing right under a cherry
tree. You know how much I love cherries, right? I'm going
right under a cherry tree and eating cherries off the tree at
the same time. I am simultaneously fertilising the tree and
eating from it! How are you not laughing?

Enter Jan: limping and covered in black soot.

–   (*Jan.*) Where are you?

–   (*Soldier looks up to the sky.*) There go the starlings.
A flock of starlings! That is so awesome! (*A shadow
suddenly cast over him.*) No wait, those aren't starlings…
those are Phantoms… they're ours, Mum… look! You can
tell by the Star of David on the side of the plane, see that?
They're Phantoms! '*Hear, Israel! The Lord is our God, the
Lord is one!*' (*The Phantom planes start dropping bombs.*)
What are you doing?! Mummy! What are they doing?!

–   (*Jan.*) IK HOU VAN JE[31] –

–   They are one of us! Soldier, hold your fire! Mum! They're
one of us!

*A violin plays against the backdrop of the bombing
campaign. The soldier laughs.*

–   I've given birth to a soldier! I've given birth to a soldier!

–   He won't be a soldier. He will go to the University of
Amsterdam and study all about Ancient China, human
rights, classical studies, musicology…

–   He will be a soldier,

–   He will *not* be a soldier!!!

–   He'll want to be a soldier.

–   He'll want to be a cellist.

---

31. I love you.

- Linguist.

- Water engineer.

- Dancer?

- He'll want to be in uniform.

- Over my dead body.

- Wrap himself in the flag.

- Over our six million dead bodies.

5.

2.30 a.m. A sleepless night.

- They took her to Auschwitz.

- Who, Bertien?

- Yeah, Bertien. They took her to Auschwitz. Took her to Auschwitz and he lost the plot.

- Who did?

- Went crazy, missing her –

- Went crazy with guilt.

- Went crazy from all the sneaking around; on his wife; Resistance fighter, Ingrid van Heugten.

- But that Jew, Bertien. She was his everything.

- Fine.

- That Jewess; she meant everything to him, did she?

- She did. And she was pregnant. By him.

- She was pregnant, that's right. In Auschwitz.

–   She went to Auschwitz, pregnant and he was going crazy with worry; with anxiety; desperate to save her and the baby.

–   Because he had no children by her, Ingrid van Heugten, that is –

–   The landlady –

–   Yes, the landlady. His wife. He had no children by her.

–   And he wanted children. Especially during the war. Life is precious and people realise they do actually want children.

–   And his wife, she didn't…?

–   I found this stuffed in one the nooks in the walls.

–   What's this –

–   An *Erika 8*.

–   The Nazis used to type on these.

–   What, in Amsterdam?

–   Amsterdam is –

–   Not like Berlin.

–   Not like Warsaw.

–   You won't see her stripping round here.

–   Who?

–   She doesn't walk these streets shouting out stuff in Yiddish.

–   She?

–   The Holocaust.

–   Over here, she floats. All thin and translucent.

–   Like the train of a bridal gown.

–   Or a veil.

–   Floats? What, like some sort of milk crust over the canals?

–   More like an inflamed tear duct.

–   I can hear her laugh. A feminine, woman's laughter.

–   A woman who knows how beautiful she was –

–   Beautiful? The Holocaust?

–   I can feel her. Mevrouw van Heugten. I can feel her sweat, her terror.

–   It's her hiding place.

–   I become one with her. With the building; the city; the whole world.

–   You think you know who you are? Go on, ask him.

–   He's sleeping.

–   You think you really know who you are, huh? Really and truly. Genetically. Biblically. Step right in. Come inside.

–   Inside where?

–   Inside my burrow.

–   In here?

–   Come inside.

–   He's still in love with you.

–   It's collective guilt is what it is.

–   He's drawn to you.

–   Vile philo-Semite.

–   Look at the way he's got his hand right over your belly.

–   He does love his Jews, doesn't he? And his gypsies too. Loves his blacks, and people whose skin reeks of bold-coloured spices.

–   He loves how they need him.

–   He loves how their palms perspire.

–   He comes inside my burrow.

–   He loves it when it's damp.

6.

4 a.m. Inside the burrow.

–   I am here.

–   In the burrow?

–   Where else then?

–   Outside, on the canals, in the streets, the flowers. On our bridge over the Keizersgracht. At Museum Square, like everyone else. A pint of local lager in hand. Some paper cone either stuffed with chips or super-skunk.

–   It's only the epidermis.

–   The burrow?

–   It's the core. Where her DNA lies.

–   The burrow?

–   This is where the maggots form.

–   I am in awe of your totality.

–   You know that film about that actor?

–   A small door, just like this one, takes whoever walks through it right inside their own head.

–   You get inside your head.

–   Your seed.

–   Your semen?

–   The seed of creation.

–   He wants to go in.

–   Not now.

–   But why?

–   Not now.

–   Why though?

–   Someone's already in there.

– Who?

– Her husband.

– Her husband?

– Meneer van Heugten. He's a turncoat.

– Meneer van Heugten? A turncoat?

– A turncoat, right.

– He walks into the local bar; the local bar that's swarming with Gestapo officers –

– Swarming!

– Swarming, yes. All Gestapo officers. And on this folded-up beer coaster he writes down, '289 Keizersgracht, Amsterdam'.

– 289 Keizersgracht, and underneath, adds the name 'Ingrid van Heugten'.

– His own wife.

– Yes. Cos he's been thinking about it for weeks. For weeks now, he's been driving himself crazy, trying to figure out a way to get her back from there; Bertien.

– He's selling out his wife.

– He's writing his wife's name down, Ingrid van Heugten, and their address: 289 Keizersgracht, Amsterdam on his beer coaster and pops it in, yeah? He stuffs into the Gestapo officer's black, furry coat pocket, at the local bar. And whispers, 'Resistance men are hiding out there.'

– He's giving her address.

– The violinist's address?

– She's at 289 Keizersgracht, Amsterdam, right?

– Right.

– Her address then.

–   On the condition they locate his little Jewish piglet and deliver her right back into his arms.

–   Precisely. That is the condition. That is the condition.

–   While he himself just takes off.

–   They'll not survive without him.

–   No way.

–   Obviously not.

–   And then, his wife; Mevrouw van Heugten, she gets hauled off to Auschwitz whereas his Jewish lover –

–   Bertien.

–   Bertien they let go. In exchange for – what was it, four... five... six members of the Resistance?

–   Turncoat piece of scum.

–   'Righteous Among the Nations' my arse.

–   They're kicking our door in. Our door. The front door of our home.

–   The door you open to go to work.

–   The door you open to go to the market for some fresh salmon from the North Sea and some asparagus stalks, paying in euros and saying 'Doei' to the stall owners in the sweetest little foreign girl's Dutch.

–   The door you wrote '*Here live...*' on in Dutch; in your own handwriting. How d'you spell 'wonen'[32] anyway?

–   The door you open to go down the stairs with your bin liner and the envelope that's got your niece's address on it and the word 'ISRAEL' written in all caps; where you've stuffed a tiny spoon and a little Dutch cow made of baked Fimo you'd picked up at this small shop on the Waterlooplein.

–   They have an exact address and they know what they're after.

---

32. Dutch for 'live'.

– They're kicking the door in and are heading straight for this room. Mevrouw van Heugten and three other Resistance men sleep in here.

– Here, in our bedroom, where we put up those Kandinsky prints we'd picked up at the Museum of Modern Art in Dubrovnik.

– Here, in our bedroom, where we have that photo of us kissing on the boat on the canals at Pride.

– Here, in our bedroom, where we did poppers the moment before the mother of all climaxes.

– And Meneer van Heugten?

– He's not here.

– He's not?

– It so happens that he isn't around tonight. It so happens that tonight he won't be sleeping at home. He's telling his wife he's gotta go off somewhere to umm... –

– Arnhem.

– Arnhem?

– Arnhem or Zwolle, whichever. Point is, he's going away on business.

– That's what he's telling her.

– And she's staying here. Sleeping. In our bed.

– Pause –

– The longest –

– Ever.

– (*Scream.*) Nothing there!!!

– They're after the rats that are hiding in the burrows –

– In the walls; the drainpipes –

– Those rats!

– Those subhumans.

– They come bursting into the flat, waving their nightsticks about, hauling off Mevrouw van Heugten and charging into this room, right here, kicking the door in and discovering the first burrow. They take the people away –

– Some they shoot right in the head –

– Whoever they feel like –

– Yeah.

– And that's it.

– What d'you mean, that's it?

– That's it.

– They don't destroy all the other nooks and burrows?

– No. Why would they do that?

– Well, to keep others from using them.

– Nah, why bother? They just stay in the flat and live there.

– Your flat.

– The flat that you chose out of all the flats you'd been to see in all of Amsterdam's coolest neighbourhoods.

– The flat over the canal. Because you love the echoing of your wooden heels, don't you? Clicking along the canal sidewalk.

– The flat – where you keep your granny-bike locked right by the front door with this lock you've learned to open with just the one hand. Even when you've got gloves on.

– The flat whose rooms you were going in and out of, laptop in hand, giving your friends back in Israel a Skype tour.

– The flat where you learnt to bake Dutch speculaas with cinnamon, cardamom, and cloves and came knocking on your neighbour, old man Jan's door, tray of cookies in hand, but he wouldn't answer the door; oh no, he wouldn't

answer the door even when he was sat in his living room
playing Jacques Brel's greatest hits on an old gramophone.

–   *Your* flat is being claimed by the regime. They work there.
     And sleep there. And eat there.

–   Using the gas.

–   Using the gas to boil their fucking water.

–   Using the gas to warm up their putrid bodies.

–   Using the gas to fry up their heathen pork chops.

–   Mmm… lekker[33] –

–   Cunts.

–   In your own home.

–   The cunting cunts!

–   And never paying the bill.

–   In your own home where you've always thought, 'What if
     Jews used to hide in here?'

–   Nazis lived in your own home!!!

–   Didn't see that one coming, did you?

–   Nazis!!!

–   Pause!

–   Nazis!!!

–   Pause!!!!!!

–   Pause, pause.

---

33. Dutch for 'yummy'.

7.

3.25 a.m. Going into labour in the bedroom.

– And then what?

– And then the Jewess, Bertien, is home from Auschwitz.

– And by the looks of her – well, what's left of her, you can see –

– That fetus inside her is still alive.

– The fetus is still alive?!

– And she's due any day now. Having their baby.

– Right here. Right here in this room. On this bed.

– But there are Nazis living in this house!

– True, but during the day, when the Nazis are off Naziiing about, she lets herself back in the flat; she, Bertien, along with Meneer van Heugten, let themselves in so that they can grab some of their stuff.

– Grab her clothes that she'd stuffed in the walls.

– Grab her papers that she'd stashed in the burrows.

– Grab her cameras.

– Cameras?

– That's right, she's got cameras. They documented everything, the books and the burrows, and they come to take their cameras, and then –

– 'I'm just going to sit down on this bed for a second – '

– She says.

– No, that was me.

– 'I feel it's time. It's time – '

– She says.

– No, that was me! Me!

- Meaning what?
- Meaning me.
- Meaning what?
- Meaning it's time.
- Time for what?
- It's *time*!
- Aaaarrrggghhh!!!!
- Six short breaths! Come on!
- Hfff... hfff... hfff... hfff... hfff... hfff...

8.

4.22 a.m. Hospital. Monitor.

- Di!!![34]
- Who's she saying that to?
- Di!!!
- Di!!!
- She wants her baby to die?!
- Mummy! Mummy!
- Mummy's not here, baby girl. Mummy's far, far away.
- Push –
- Push –
- Push –
- Push –
- Mind your farts –
- In Europe, we give birth gracefully.

---

34. Pronounced 'dye' – Hebrew for 'Enough/no more!'

9.

– And then they take her away.

– Her?

– Her, they take her away. The Nazis take her back, and the baby they leave behind.

– They take her back?

– And the baby, they leave behind. *The darkness no one wants to talk about*

– Her, they take back to Auschwitz, and the baby they leave behind. That's right, the baby they just leave on the bed, in the flat, in that room in the flat; that room in *your* flat where you change your spotless, speckless baby's pastel, tetra nappies you'd picked up for him at some babywear shop over on De Pijp. They leave her alone on that bed because they know she'll die. They know she'll die in a way we can't even bring ourselves to imagine.

– No, we can't even bring ourselves to imagine that!

– Cos it's a baby –

– Cos it's a baby –

– Cos it's a baby –

– But for the Nazis, she wasn't a baby.

– She was a maggot.

– A what now?

– A maggot. She was no more than a maggot.

– And maggots you can squish with the heel of your shoe.

– Maggots you can gas with insecticide.

– ISIS –

– What in the world has ISIS got to do with anything?!

– Dunno… my mind just suddenly went, 'ISIS'.

10.

5.47 a.m. At home. Cradling baby in arms.

- (*Smeared in blood.*) War's over.

- Just in time.

- In time?

- Just in time. Because Mevrouw van Heugten is still alive. The war's about to be over. And she's still alive.

- The Nazis have left her flat.

- Scurried off like a pack of rats.

- Like a pack of bottom-feeders.

- Like a pack of degenerates.

- Scurried off like a pack of degenerates. And Mevrouw van Heugten –

- Has made it back from Auschwitz.

- Back here. To this room. This door.

- This floor.

- These walls.

- She's come back here. To your flat, yeah, she's back; let herself in, and what's she doing now?

- Is she reaching out to those three, four, five Resistance men her husband had ratted out?

- Yeah, she's reaching out to them. And, she's reaching out to him too.

- Him?

- Her husband.

- She's reaching out to him?

- She's telling him she's forgiven him.

- She's forgiven him because…? She's forgiven him for…? She's forgiven him? How?

–   No. She hasn't forgiven him. She hasn't forgiven him at
    all. Not in the slightest. She's only telling him she's
    forgiven him and now she's asking him to come home.
    And anyway, it's not as if he's forgiven himself.

–   He's come back to tell her that.

–   But he doesn't tell her that, does he? He comes home and
    doesn't tell her that at all. He comes home and she's not
    even there. Instead –

–   Instead, he finds two men there; two Resistance men. And
    they have him sit down; right here, in this chair.

–   He sits in this chair, right. And…?

–   And drinks from the glass they give him.

–   Glass of, what, jenever?

–   It is a jenever glass, yes, but what's in it, that's not jenever.
    He knows what's in that glass. He knows full well what's
    inside that glass and he knows he's had it coming. He
    knows the Resistance playbook.

–   So he downs it. No bargaining.

–   It takes, what, two, three minutes?

–   Two.

–   Two minutes. And that's that.

–   That's that.

–   Just the way they like to do things over here. Clean.
    Quick. Clean.

–   The end?

–   No. That's not the end. Because he's not dead. Meneer van
    Heugten isn't dead. Even after he'd sold out his own wife
    to the Nazis; even after he'd sold out three Resistance
    fighters to the Nazis; even after he'd sold out all these
    people to the Nazis; still, no one would look at him as this
    base, loathsome, immoral slug of a man, because he

happened to save the woman he loved, and that woman so happened to be a Jew.

–   All hail the Righteous Among the Nations!

–   He's alive?

–   He's not dead, because he knew.

–   He knew, that's right. He knew she wouldn't forgive him. Because he knows his wife.

–   He knew they'd be waiting. He knew the Resistance playbook. He wrote the Resistance playbook.

–   He believed in the Resistance playbook.

–   And he knew.

–   Oh yeah, he knew that wasn't jenever.

–   He knew it was –

–   Sodium thiopental –

–   Vecuronium bromide –

–   Potassium chloride –

–   But he downed it like a man.

–   Downed it like a man's man –

–   He downed it like he was owning up to all of it; the deception, the love, the betrayal, all of it.

–   But he wouldn't die, would he? Forty-three whole minutes. And he wouldn't die.

–   Okay, forty-three whole minutes during which he was what, convulsing to death?

–   Yeah. 5.52 p.m. he started to convulse. All the way till 6.35 p.m. Forty-three whole minutes during which he was twitching, writhing, moaning, groaning –

–   Drooling –

–   Yeah, drooling; drooling, and foaming –

– Foaming; what like, foaming at the mouth?

– Yeah, he was foaming at the mouth. And with all that foam; with all that foam he had gushing out of his mouth, he still somehow managed to talk.

– He did talk, that's right. Talked about his childhood; how no one ever really saw him; never saw his pain; never saw his loneliness.

– His loneliness, his otherness, yeah... and it was because of all that, right? Cos of all that, that he developed that strong sense of identification with all those minorities.

– So strong was his sense of identification with all those minorities that he went ahead and studied law so that he could represent all those subhuman fuckwits and degenerates.

– And it was because of that, that he ended up falling for a Jew; and saving her.

– He was vomiting too.

– Vomiting, and drooling; oh, and he also lost control of all his bodily functions.

– Had lost all control of all his bodily functions and even though he had no control of any of his orifices, even though that was the case, he still tried to get up.

– Too right he did. Tried to get up several times, three or four times.

– Fourteen. Fourteen times he tried to get up –

– And he fell down –

– And he convulsed –

– And he apologised –

– He did not apologise. No. He got up, and fell down, did his little convulsing routine; pissed himself fourteen times, forty-three minutes straight, but there was no apology. No, sir. There was a lot of explaining, and describing, and emoting, but no apologies.

– He's not the apologising kind. He's more the 'drink-the-mock-jenever-you're-served-like-a-man-who-can-own-up-to-his-decisions' kind. He's the kind to down his drink like a man who knows how to own up to his decisions and convulse to death until his muscles are all atrophied and have ceased all motor functions.

– Until he's gone limp.

– Until his heart succumbs to all the toxins.

– And the body?

– The body was dumped. Oh yeah, they dumped his body; dumped it where?

– Here.

– Here. Right here. Out the window of your Keizersgracht flat.

– Your canal-facing window.

– The window facing the canal you like to watch through strands of rain whilst mulling over your partiture that's due the following week.

– Through the window, yes; the one framing everything that's nothing to do with your own childhood. That's the one.

– The window overlooking the Kaiser's canal. Your favourite canal out of all of them. The canal with the little bridge over it where you fell in love.

– That canal, right, which'll be the very first thing your child sees that first time they come out of the house.

– Which you will walk across every rain-free morning, whisper-humming your Hebrew nursery rhymes.

– Ken La'zipor Bein Ha'ezeem[35] –

– On the canal, the Kaiser's canal. Just under the bridge.

– No!

---

35. 'There sits a bird's nest amidst the trees.'

- Under the bridge.

- No, anything but under the bridge...

- But that's the way it happened. They dumped his body under the bridge.

- Under the bridge? Our bridge?

- Under our bridge. On the Keizersgracht.

- I am a common starling.

- Right here, under our bridge? On the Keizersgracht.

- Kut.[36]

- The end?

- No. Not the end. It isn't the end because he isn't dead.

- He isn't dead. He's not the dying kind. He only played dead. He only played dead and he made sure he injected himself with the antidote to whatever concoction was inside that so-called glass of jenever he knew they'd have ready for him.

- He injected himself with the antidote, that's right; because he knew exactly the type of compound that was going to be in there, because he wrote their playbook, he came up with the Resistance code; came up with the punishment for traitors; he came up with everything. Everything he turned against, everything he was forced to turn against, all of it was his brainchild. So he made sure he injected himself ahead of time, and he played dead when they dumped him in the canal. He went under and waited.

- He waited. That's right. He waited. Went under and waited.

- Went under and waited?

- Went under. The man dived under two blocks' worth of canals, just like that; with all that sodium thiopental, vecuronium bromide and potassium chloride coursing

---

36. From Dutch: an exclamation one makes when something bad or annoying's happened, e.g. 'shit', 'damn'...

through his system, just like that; dived under and across the canals and when he got to the Lauriergracht, yes, it was at the Lauriergracht where he finally stuck his head out of the water and waited in the dark; under a small bridge. He was waiting for –

– He was waiting for them – his executioners, to leave. To get out of the flat. And then he went back.

– Went back?

– He went back to the flat; his flat; the one above; the one that's above yours; his flat.

– Jan's?

– Yours and Jan's used to be the one flat, originally. So yeah, he went back to his and Ingrid van Heugten's flat, and the one downstairs – yours that is – he rented out. And upstairs; yes, upstairs, the flat upstairs, that's where he lives. To this day.

– Jan? van Heugten?

– Jan; Jan van Heugten. Living up there to this very day. Sipping his jenever as we speak; watching some *Spelling Bee* on the television and playing his Jacques Brel records.

– And is he…?

– He is. He absolutely is.

– Not paying that bill?

– He's not paying that bill.

The End.

A Nick Hern Book

Amsterdam first published as a paperback original in Great Britain in 2019 by Nick Hern Books Limited, The Glasshouse, 49a Goldhawk Road, London W12 8QP, in association with the Orange Tree Theatre, Richmond, Actors Touring Company and Theatre Royal Plymouth

Amsterdam copyright © 2019 Maya Arad Yasur

Maya Arad Yasur has asserted her right to be identified as the author of this work

Cover image designed by Nick Hern Books from an architect's rendering of Algemene Boekhandel J.H. van Heeteren, Hartenstraat, Amsterdam, 1887

Designed and typeset by Nick Hern Books, London
Printed in the UK by Mimeo Ltd, Huntingdon, Cambridgeshire PE29 6XX

A CIP catalogue record for this book is available from the British Library

ISBN 978 1 84842 889 8

www.nickhernbooks.co.uk

facebook.com/nickhernbooks

twitter.com/nickhernbooks